Changing Sources of U.S. Economic Growth, 1950-2010

A Chartbook of Trends and Projections

Nestor E. Terleckyj

National Planning Association

Changing Sources of U.S. Economic Growth, 1950-2010
A Chartbook of Trends and Projections

NPA Report #244

Price $15.00

ISBN 0-89068-101-5
Library of Congress Catalog Card Number 89-64097

Printed in the United States of America

 C439

Contents

Dramatic changes—demographic, social and economic—are projected to occur in the United States during the next two decades. These changes may threaten economic growth if not countered quickly and effectively through private and public policies. The population is aging, the labor force is not likely to increase much from additional two-family earners, and we face keen international competition.

This Chartbook presents past and future trends in an examination of the timing and magnitude of these economic and demographic changes and the relationships among them that influence per capita income. Its conclusions are graphic and, I believe, very significant.

It shows that future U.S. economic growth in the aggregate and in per capita income will depend largely on the future growth of U.S. productivity (output per worker). Thus, it will be critical to maintain levels of investment in factors that contribute to productivity growth, specifically, modern fixed capital, training and education, public infrastructure, and the development and effective use of new technologies. Maintaining a general climate favorable for such investments, supported by specific policies to achieve them, must be a top priority for the future. These policies require maintaining overall economic stability and avoiding deep recessions such as those of the mid-1970s and early 1980s.

The Chartbook does not attempt to outline specific policy prescriptions or to predict the exact shape in which problems will occur. It does, however, portray the types of potential problems and the general nature of actions that will be required to sustain reasonable economic growth.

The charts demonstrate dramatically that the difference between success and failure can be a change of only 1 percent per year in productivity growth. Failure during the next 20 years to raise productivity above the sluggish 0.8 percent growth rate of the past two decades could lead to serious economic and social problems that would make closing the fiscal deficit or the international trade deficit extremely difficult. Failure to raise productivity would also be very costly in terms of individual well-being, serious social conflicts between classes and generations, and impeding requisite changes.

In contrast, a productivity growth rate on the order of 1.2 to 1.5 percent a year and the avoidance of deep recessions would permit a successful management of change over the next two decades.

We have time to meet the problem and to put this nation on a course of sustained growth that would provide comfortable real incomes for retirees and opportunities for economic advancement for the young while facilitating the internal adjustments requisite to a changing world economy.

The question is whether we have the foresight and the will to take advantage of this window of opportunity.

John T. Dunlop
Lamont University Professor, Emeritus
Harvard University

Acknowledgments

This Chartbook was prepared as an NPA internal research project. The members and the staff of the NPA Board of Trustees' Committee on the Enhancement of Human Resources reviewed several intermediate drafts and made numerous substantive comments and suggestions.

I would like to acknowledge with appreciation the detailed comments and suggestions on the draft of this report made by Ronald E. Kutscher, Bureau of Labor Statistics, Department of Labor, and Jack E. Triplett, Bureau of Economic Analysis, Department of Commerce.

I have received valuable advice and assistance in assembling consistent sets of U.S. government data that most closely correspond to the desired concepts. In particular, I would like to thank Edwin R. Dean, Bureau of Labor Statistics; W. Vance Grant, Office of Educational Research and Improvement, Department of Education; William Gullickson and John Stinson, Bureau of Labor Statistics; and Gregory Spencer, Bureau of the Census, Department of Commerce.

Charles D. Coleman performed the numerous economic growth model simulations reflected in this report and prepared the graphic presentations.

The author alone is responsible for the choice of projection assumptions and for any errors that may remain.

Nestor E. Terleckyj

About the Author

Nestor E. Terleckyj is a Vice President of the National Planning Association and President of NPA Data Services, Inc. He holds a Ph.D. degree in economics from Columbia University and is the author of several books and numerous articles in the fields of economic growth, productivity and economics of technical change. Dr. Terleckyj has previously held professional positions with the U.S. Office of Management and Budget, the Conference Board and the National Bureau of Economic Research, Inc.

C hanges are under way in the composition of the U.S. population and in the U.S. and global economies that will radically affect the rate of economic growth in the United States. Although private and public policies may change several of the key variables, the direction of many of these changes is firmly set.

Over the past 40 years, economic well-being as measured by gross national product per capita has grown, but the sources of this growth have changed significantly. In the 1950s and 1960s, per capita income increased as a consequence of productivity growth. Population and employment grew at the same rate, and the increased output per worker generated growth in earnings per worker.

In the 1970s and early 1980s, output and earnings per worker became stagnant. Most of the per capita economic growth during that time resulted from an increased percentage of the population (largely women) entering the paid workforce. Benefits that accrued to households with additional workers were not as evenly distributed as they would have been through price adjustments or higher compensation, the traditional means of distributing productivity increases.

Since 1983, there has been modest growth in productivity. It is too early to tell whether this upturn marks the beginning of a long-term revival or is a short-term phenomenon caused by the absence of major recessions.

By the turn of the century, growth in the proportion of the working population—which, as noted, accounted for most of the progress in economic well-being over the past two decades—will decline to less than 1 percent a year and then become negative. Only limited growth in the number of new workers can be expected from either increased immigration or delayed retirements. Unless productivity growth rates revive, economic growth in the United States will stall and perhaps cease entirely early in the next century.

Whether and how per capita income growth can be sustained over the next 20 years are the critical questions for private and public policy analysis and planning.

This Chartbook depicts trends in population, labor force and capital formation (including fixed capital, human capital, public infrastructure, and technology) as they affect the outlook for U.S. productivity and economic growth in the decades ahead. It outlines the possible consequences for future economic growth of a repetition of the large business cycle fluctuations of the 1974-82 period and examines the implications for future U.S. standards of living of different productivity growth patterns.

The data and analyses were drawn largely from earlier work of the National Economic Projections Series produced by NPA, and more recently by NPA Data Services, Inc., and from previous NPA research by the author on the economics of technology and productivity. The charts reflect data available through July 1989. Selection of topics and mode of presentation were dictated by the aims of highlighting the relation of individual trends and economic growth and of identifying the degree of uncertainty in the relationships.

The time frame for this analysis covers the past 40 years and the outlook for the next 20. A "Technical Note" is appended to describe the methods and sources used. Specific sources and explanations are provided in the notes to individual charts. The basic data series for historical periods and the current baseline projection from the National Economic Projections Series are provided in the statistical tables.

POPULATION,
LABOR FORCE
AND EMPLOYMENT

The steady decline in the birth rate has reduced the population growth rate for future generations.

The birth rate has continued to fall since its drop in the 1960s (Chart 1). This decline has slowed population growth and, as a result, the average age of the population has been increasing. The birth rate is expected to remain low and to decrease even further.

The death rate has also declined, extending life expectancy and contributing to the aging of the population.

Chart 1

Birth and Death Rates in the United States as a Percentage of January 1 Population, 1950-2010

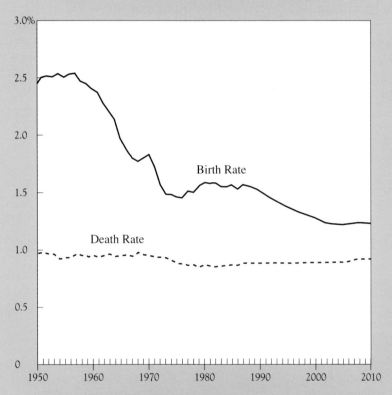

Note: The Census projections have been adjusted to reflect a higher immigration rate and to conform to actual U.S. population data through July 1989.

Sources: 1950-1988 (Actual): U.S. Department of Commerce, Bureau of the Census. 1989-2010: Projections by NPA Data Services based on the Census Bureau's middle fertility and middle mortality assumptions, published in Gregory Spencer, *Projections of the Population of the United States by Age, Sex, and Race: 1988 to 2080*, Series P-25, Report No. 1018 (Washington, D.C.: U.S. Department of Commerce, Bureau of the Census, 1989).

Large increases in life expectancy have occurred in the 20th century.

Life span increased dramatically throughout the world in the 20th century. In the United States, life expectancy at birth for men and women combined rose by nearly 20 years during the period 1901-50— from 49.3 years to 68.2 years. Gains in life span continued after 1950, with an additional 7.2 years for women and 5.7 years for men between 1950 and 1985 (Chart 2).

Further increases are likely. The Census Bureau indicates gains of 3.2 years for men and 3.1 years for women between 1985 and 2010.

Reductions in mortality from heart disease and stroke have significantly increased the life span of older people. Since 1950, gains at age 65 have continued to represent a rising proportion of the increase in life span at birth.

Chart 2

Life Expectancy in the United States, at Birth and at Age 65, 1950-2010

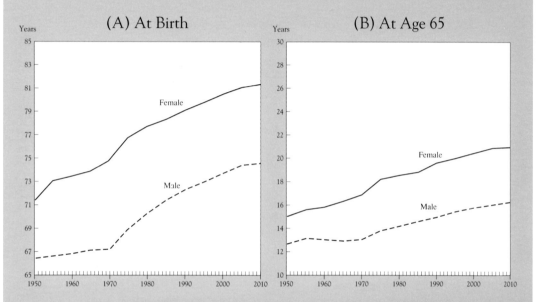

(A) At Birth

(B) At Age 65

Note: Life expectancy is calculated from the mortality rates of different age and sex categories in a given year. Life expectancy at birth in a given year reflects mortality rates in that year at all ages. Projections for years after 1985 are based on the middle mortality assumption used in the 1989 Census Bureau projections.

Source: (A) and (B): Gregory Spencer, *Projections of the Population of the United States by Age, Sex, and Race: 1988 to 2080*, Series P-25, Report No. 1018 (Washington, D.C.: Bureau of the Census, 1989).

By 2010, immigration will likely become as important a source of U.S. population growth as the resident population increase.

Immigration to the United States has risen as global communications and travel have improved and political instabilities have continued to trouble different areas of the world. The sources of immigration to the United States have become much more diversified and now include practically all countries.

The immigration rate is less predictable than U.S. birth and death rates. Assuming a constant immigration rate, based on the proportion of immigrants to resident population in 1985, immigration will almost equal the natural increase of the U.S. population by 2010 (Chart 3). Current data support the expectation that the rate of immigration will at least remain constant rather than decline in the future.

The 1989 Census projections indicate zero and probably negative population growth by the time newborns in 1990 reach age 40. It is also quite likely that when these individuals are 25 years old, the primary source of population growth will be immigration rather than the natural increase in the resident population.

Because immigrants to the United States are generally younger than the resident population, their contribution to the growth of the labor force will probably be somewhat larger and occur earlier than their contribution to the total population.

Chart 3

Sources of U.S. Population Growth, 1950-2010

Thous.

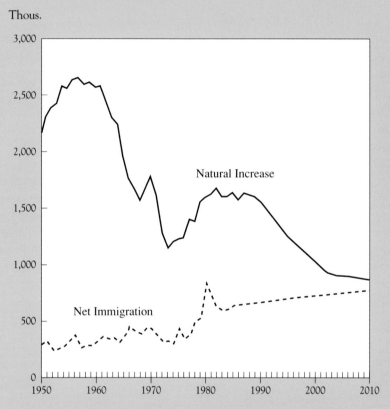

Note: The Census projections have been adjusted to reflect a higher immigration rate and to conform to actual U.S. population data through July 1989.

Sources: 1950-1988 (Actual): Bureau of the Census. 1989-2010: Projections by NPA Data Services based on the Census Bureau's middle fertility and middle mortality assumptions, published in Gregory Spencer, *Projections of the Population of the United States by Age, Sex, and Race: 1988 to 2080*, Series P-25, Report No. 1018 (Washington, D.C.: Bureau of the Census, 1989).

The labor force will continue to grow at a higher rate than the population for the next 20 years.

Between 1950 and 1969, population, labor force and employment grew at an average annual rate of 1.5 percent. In the 1970s, labor force and employment growth accelerated to 2.4 percent, while population growth slowed to 1.1 percent.

Due to the large population of young workforce entrants in the 1970s and 1980s who reflected the delayed effects of the 1946-60 baby boom as well as the rising participation rates of women, the labor force expanded much more rapidly in percentage terms than the overall population.

Between 1969 and 1979, the total number employed (including the armed forces) increased at an annual rate 1.1 percent greater than the rate of population growth. This difference between employment and population growth dropped to 0.7 percent per year in the 1979-89 period.

Allowing for projected increases in the participation rates of women and older workers and for a small decline in long-term unemployment, the differential growth of employment over population may average 0.6 percent to the year 2000, continue at that rate in the 2000-05 period, and fall to 0.4 percent during 2005-10.

Chart 4

Annual Increases in the U.S. Population and Labor Force, 1950-2010

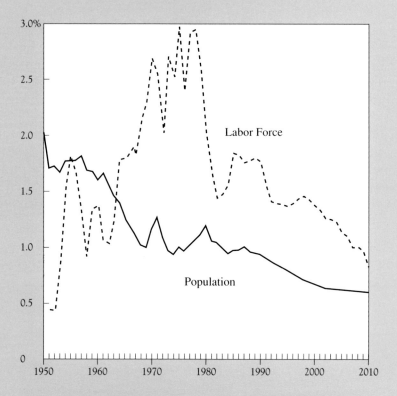

Note: Annual changes in the labor force were converted to three-year moving averages to highlight long-term trends.

Sources: 1950-1988 (Actual): Total population as reported by the Bureau of the Census; total civilian labor force as reported by U.S. Department of Labor, Bureau of Labor Statistics (BLS). 1989-2010 (Predicted): NPA Data Services, Inc.

The rising participation rates of women have been a main factor in the growth of the U.S. labor force. These increases are now slowing.

The increasing participation rates of women in the labor force since the mid-1960s are due to a number of factors. The decline in the birth rate has helped to make careers outside the home easier for women; educational attainment levels of women have risen; the nature of many work opportunities has changed; and political and social norms have changed as well.

The projections of the labor force participation rates of women take into account the number of children born to women of different ages and the extent of the college experience of different aged women. The projections indicate continued increases in the participation rates of women, but at progressively smaller increments as they approach the participation rates of men (Chart 5).

Chart 5

Civilian Labor Force Participation Rates, Ages 25-34 and 35-44, 1950-2010

(A) Age 25-34   (B) Age 35-44

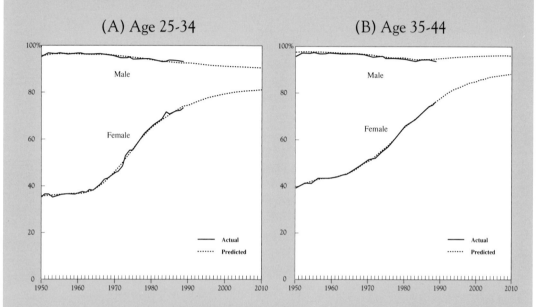

Sources: (A) and (B) 1950-1988 (Actual): Civilian labor force
participation rates based on household survey data, BLS. 1950-2010
(Predicted): NPA Data Services, Inc.

By continuing to work, Americans in the 55-64 age group may ease future labor supply and federal budget pressures.

There are indications of future increases in the participation rates of older workers. A reversal of the decline in the participation rates of men in the 55-64 age bracket and a rise in the rates of women in that age group (Chart 6) would contribute to increases in the employment-population ratio and alleviate the growing costs of transfer payments to the dependent population.

The participation rates of women age 55-64 are likely to increase because of rising educational levels and greater previous work experience. Although increased levels of education in this age group of men will also make longer work participation more attractive, a reverse in the decline of their participation rates is less certain.

For both men and women, an increase in life expectancy at higher ages and uncertainty about long-term means of support, including the future value of government benefits, are likely to provide incentives for continuing paid employment.

Chart 6

Civilian Labor Force Participation Rates, Age 55-64, 1950-2010

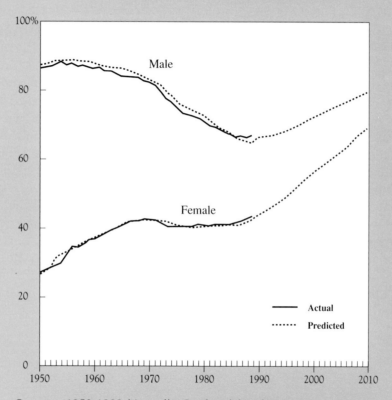

Sources: 1950-1988 (Actual): Civilian labor force participation rates based on household survey data, BLS. 1950-2010 (Predicted): NPA Data Services, Inc.

The working-age population will continue to increase until 2010. The share of the dependent-age population will then increase, but its age composition will change.

For the next 20 years, the dependency ratio—the population under 18 and 65 and older relative to the working-age population—will continue to decline (Chart 7). This is one factor contributing to the continued growth of the labor force at a rate higher than that of population. But the proportion of the dependent-age population can be expected to increase after 2010, contributing to a slowdown in labor force growth. Furthermore, the composition of this group will change significantly.

The number of young dependents has been declining since 1960, while the number of people in the traditional retirement age bracket has risen. For the next two decades, growth in the 65 and older age bracket will be moderate, reflecting the low U.S. birth rate between 1925 and 1945. However, after 2010, the proportion of this age group in the dependent-age population will increase substantially. (The higher immigration rate assumed in the present projection would not materially alter this trend.) The scope of opportunities for managing this demographic transition will be largely determined by the investments and other provisions made in the next 20 years.

Chart 7

Percentage of Population by Age Group, 1960-2030

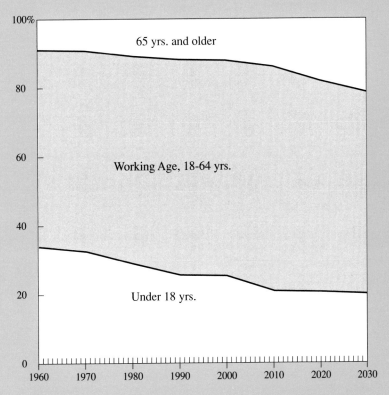

Source: Bureau of the Census.

PRODUCTIVITY,
EARNINGS
AND INCOME

The work effort of the U.S. population increased substantially in the 1970s and 1980s.

The period from 1969 to 1987 can be characterized as a period of work-based growth. The increase in the labor force participation rates of women and the decline in the dependent-age population permitted extraordinary participation rates for the total population during the 1970s and 1980s. In addition, the end of the long-term decline in hours worked per year during the 1980s contributed further to the increase in work relative to population (Chart 8). This increase is likely to continue in the future but at a diminished rate. The employment-population ratio will begin to decline after 2010 as aging of the U.S. population accelerates.

Chart 8

Indicators of the Work Effort of the U.S. Population, 1950-2010

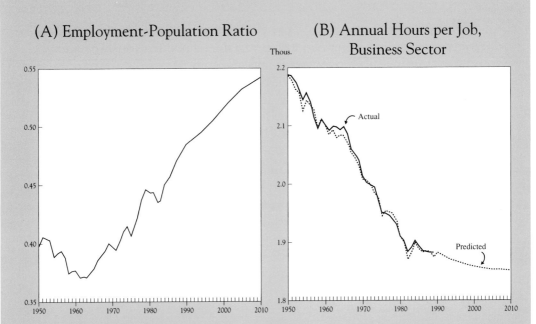

(A) Employment-Population Ratio

(B) Annual Hours per Job, Business Sector

Sources: (A) Employment-Population Ratio—1950-1988 (Actual): Average number of persons employed as reported for the year by BLS divided by the total U.S. population as reported for July 1 by the Bureau of the Census. 1989-2010 (Predicted): NPA Data Services, Inc.

(B) Annual Hours per Job—1950-1988 (Actual): BLS. Hours of all persons engaged in the private sector (including proprietors and unpaid family members) divided by total private sector employment based on establishment data. Data on hours, derived from the survey of business establishments, usually reflect hours paid. 1950-2010 (Predicted): NPA Data Services, Inc.

Output and real earnings per worker revived modestly in the 1980s after stagnating in the 1970s.

The growth of real earnings per worker is determined more by productivity than by any other economic variable. This relationship can be seen by examining GNP per worker and earnings per worker (Chart 9) and, at a more detailed level, output per hour and earnings per hour in the private business sector. Historically, the proportion of earnings to total output has fluctuated within narrow limits; since the early 1950s, it has been between 57 and 61 percent of GNP.

Output and real earnings per worker grew rapidly in the 1950s and 1960s but stagnated in the 1970s. Since the 1982 recession, both have continued a moderate rise. Although U.S. productivity growth slowed during the 1965-85 period, the adverse affect of this decline on average incomes was mitigated by the large labor force and employment increases. If GNP per capita is to maintain its growth rate of the past two decades, productivity must exceed its 1969-88 growth rate to compensate for the slowdown in the growth of employment.

Chart 9

GNP per Worker and Earnings per Worker, 1950-1989
(1967 = 100)

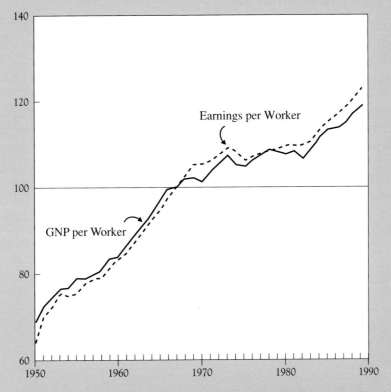

Note: Earnings (wages, salaries and other labor income) were deflated by the implicit national income deflator.

Sources: GNP in constant dollars as reported by the U.S. Department of Commerce, Bureau of Economic Analysis (BEA). Number of workers is the total number of persons employed based on household survey data as reported by BLS.

As productivity growth has slowed, labor force increases have accelerated, cushioning the drop in per capita output and income.

Growth in per capita income paralleled growth in earnings per worker until about 1970. Thereafter, until 1983, per capita income continued to increase while earnings per worker remained flat (Chart 10). The significant growth in per capita income after the productivity slowdown was due to the rising number of workers relative to population.

Growth in per capita income can be maintained in the long run only if there are increases in the employment-population ratio or in earnings per worker. Demographics show that for the next generation and beyond, sources for increases in the employment-population ratio will be exhausted. This leaves productivity growth as the impetus for future growth in earnings and per capita income. However, the future of U.S. productivity is itself uncertain.

Chart 10

Per Capita Income and Earnings per Worker,
1950-1989
(1967 = 100)

Per Capita Income

Earnings per Worker

Note: Per capita income is total personal income divided by total population; earnings per worker are total worker earnings divided by the number of persons employed. Both are deflated by the implicit national income deflator.

Sources: BEA, BLS and NPA Data Services, Inc.

PART
III

CAPITAL
FORMATION

Tangible and intangible capital formation has contributed to productivity growth, but the specific relationship of various factors to productivity changes remains elusive and poorly understood.

Productivity growth is determined by the increase in capital stocks accumulated through net investments in tangible and intangible capital. This includes capital stock generated by business investments in plant and equipment and by investments in technology derived from past expenditures for R&D in the United States and abroad; human capital stock built up by education and experience; and public capital stock derived from government expenditures for infrastructure and other long-term investments. Except for private R&D expenditures, investments in these capital stocks have been stagnant or declining for two decades.

Although subject to measurement gaps and errors as well as numerous qualifications, the data for the different capital stocks have been compiled and related to productivity changes. The results suggest direct contributions to output per worker, as in its underlying relationship to fixed nonresidential capital per hour in the private business sector (Chart 11). Despite significant uncertainties, such investment and capital data provide a more tractable means of assessing prospects for a U.S. productivity revival than intangible factors such as quality of management, working conditions and morale. While those organizational and psychological factors also affect productivity, successful quantitative assessments of them have not been obtained thus far.

Changes in productivity are also influenced by short-term fluctuations in the economy. This makes identification of specific contributions of the various factors to productivity changes even more difficult.

Chart 11

Annual Changes in Output and Fixed Nonresidential
Capital per Hour in the U.S. Business Sector,
Five-Year Moving Averages, 1950-1989

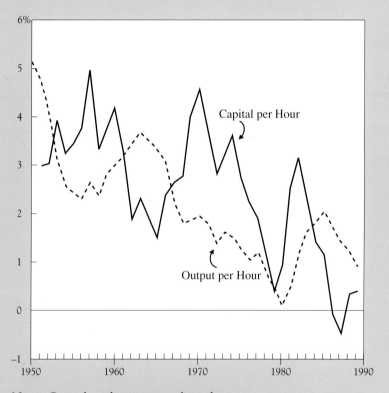

Note: Capital per hour series is lagged one year.

Sources: 1950-1986 (Actual): Real output and hours paid in the U.S.
business sector are measured by BLS. The real stock of fixed nonresidential business capital net of depreciation is measured by BEA. 1987-1989
(Predicted): NPA Data Services, Inc.

Gross fixed investment in business plant and equipment has increased over time, but net fixed private investment has continued at about the same rate since the mid-1960s.

While gross fixed nonresidential investment has continued to grow, depreciation charges have increased even faster. Consequently, net fixed private investment has not grown since the mid-1960s, but has moved cyclically without a trend (Chart 12). The rate of fixed capital formation constitutes a major uncertainty for the future. Differing trends are portrayed by gross versus net of depreciation measurements of fixed investment data, and legitimate doubts exist about the meaning and appropriateness of particular depreciation accounting methods. Nevertheless, a rising level of net fixed investment may be a more reliable indicator of prospects for future productivity improvement than the levels of gross investment.

Chart 12

Gross and Net Fixed Private Nonresidential Investment, 1950-1989

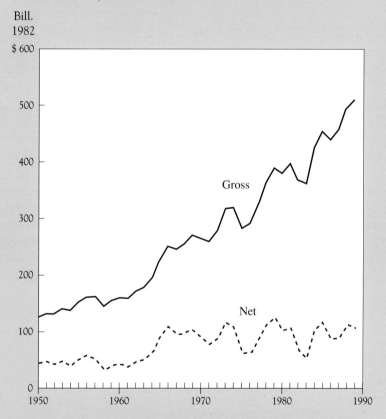

Bill.
1982

Sources: 1950-1988 (Actual): BEA. 1989 (Predicted): NPA Data Services, Inc.

Public investments in tangible infrastructure have declined
sharply since the 1960s.

Public investments in infrastructure have lagged for some time. The
level of real construction by state and local governments, which repre-
sents most of the investments in roads, airports, water and sewer systems,
and local rapid transit, is still significantly below the levels of the mid-
1960s (Chart 13).

A relatively clear relationship exists between the capital stock of
public transportation construction and the productivity increases in the
transportation sector. Estimates have been made of its impact on the
costs to consumers and to business. The economic and social consequences of neglect of other types of infrastructure investments—for
example, waste disposal—are not as evident. However, there are indications that they could be at least as important and long lasting.

If U.S. productivity growth does not improve, sluggish growth in
the tax base and large fiscal deficits will continue. In that environment,
increased government investments in infrastructure are unlikely.

Chart 13

State and Local Government Construction Expenditures, 1950-1989

Bill.
1982

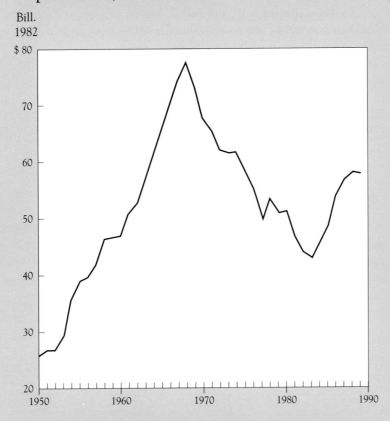

Note: Expenditures include those for highway and other projects funded by transfers from the federal government.

Sources: 1950-1988 (Actual): BEA. 1989 (Predicted): NPA Data Services, Inc.

Private R&D spending continues to grow in the United States.

Advances in technology are crucial to maintaining productivity growth. R&D investments are essential to develop new technologies and utilize those undertaken elsewhere.

Private investments in industrial R&D have continued to expand rapidly in the United States since 1950, except during a period of comparatively slow growth in the early 1970s (Chart 14). Constant dollar government spending for R&D performed in U.S. industry declined between 1965 and 1975 but began to grow rapidly after 1980, regaining its previous high.

Chart 14

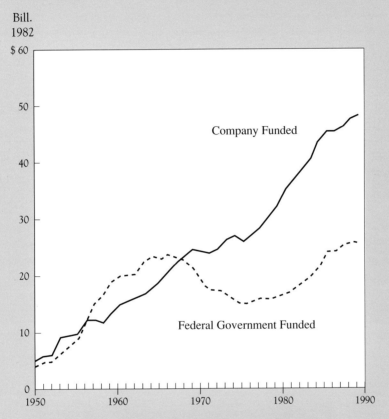

R&D Expenditures in U.S. Industry, 1950-1989

Bill. 1982

Company Funded

Federal Government Funded

Note: Expenditures are deflated by the implicit GNP deflator.

Source: National Science Foundation.

The U.S. position in world technology development continues to be strong, but other countries are increasing their share of R&D and of U.S. patents.

Private spending for R&D, the prime indicator of investments in commercial technology, has grown rapidly in the United States and Europe and very rapidly in Japan (Chart 15) and some newly industrialized countries. Since the 1950s, the foreign share of patents granted in the United States has increased steadily.

This growth in foreign technology development offers both opportunities for U.S. productivity improvements and evidence that the U.S. position in the development of new technologies is no longer as preeminent as it was in earlier decades.

Chart 15

Indicators of the U.S. Position in World Technology Development, 1950-1988

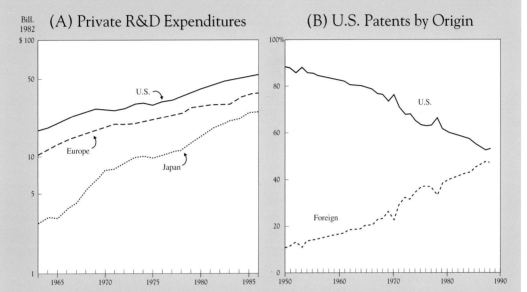

Bill. 1982

(A) Private R&D Expenditures

(B) U.S. Patents by Origin

Sources: (A) Private R&D Expenditures—1963-1983: Nestor E. Terleckyj and David M. Levy, "Trends in Industrial R&D Activities in the United States, Europe and Japan, 1963-83" (Washington, D.C.: National Planning Association, 1985), paper given at the National Bureau of Economic Research's *Conference on Economic Growth in Japan and the United States*. 1984-1986: Data series for earlier years were extended to 1986 using data from the Organization for Economic Cooperation and Development (May 1988). Data for Europe are for seven countries that undertake major R&D.

(B) U.S. Patents by Origin—1950-1988: Derived from the data for all patents granted in the United States as reported by the U.S. Department of Commerce, Office of Patents and Trademarks.

Human capital investment in education has stagnated for two decades, despite the increasing demand for a more educated workforce.

Human capital investment has been lagging for two decades, as shown by the largely stagnant high school and college completion rates (Chart 16). Attempts to measure the quality of education or educational attainment levels of individuals remain difficult to undertake and controversial. However, almost no evidence indicates that the decline in numbers has been offset by an improvement in quality. The lag in educational attainment has occurred as the occupational mix of U.S. employment is moving toward jobs requiring more education, as is indicated by the following projections of growth for different job categories:

	Annual Growth Rate 1986-2000
Managerial and professional specialists	1.8%
Technical, sales and administrative support	1.3
Precision production, craft and repair	0.8
Operators, fabricators and laborers	0.2
Service occupations	1.9
Farming, forestry and fisheries	- 0.3
All jobs	1.1

Source: Ronald E. Kutscher, "Overview and Implications of the Projections to 2000," Monthly Labor Review, U.S. Department of Labor, November 1987.

The stagnant levels of educational attainment at a time when high school and college populations have been declining indicate that the cost of education has increased and/or its benefits have declined sufficiently to affect human capital formation adversely. This outcome will diminish future economic growth and probably equality of opportunity.

Chart 16

Graduates as a Percentage of Respective
Population Group, 1950-1989

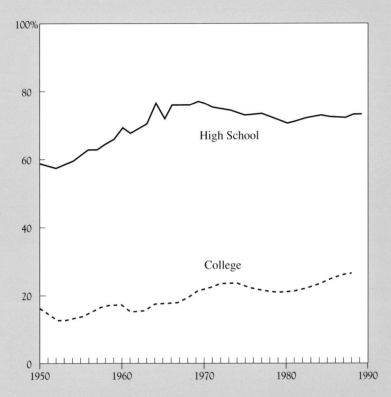

Note: The number of bachelor degrees was divided by one-fifth of the
civilian noninstitutional population age 20-24 lagged two years.

Sources: High school graduates as a percentage of the 17-year-old population for 1950-1989 and conferred bachelor degrees for 1960-1988 are from
the Office of Education Research and Improvement, U.S. Department of
Education. The data on bachelor degrees for 1950-1959 are from Nestor
E. Terleckyj, *Employment of Natural Scientists and Engineers: Recent Trends
and Prospects* (Washington, D.C.: National Planning Association, 1986).

PART
IV

LONG-TERM
OUTLOOK

Improvements in productivity growth and continued increases in per capita income appear likely until 2010 if capital investment increases and the U.S. economy can avoid deep recessions.

The investment climate created in recent years by improvements in U.S. price stability and productivity has increased the likelihood that capital investments will grow in the future. Capital investment growth combined with slower labor force growth could raise capital-labor ratios and sustain improvements in productivity growth over the next 20 years.

Despite severe recessions, productivity growth from 1979 to 1984 maintained its rates of the 1970s. The period from 1984 to 1987 witnessed continued expansion in employment and a revival in productivity growth and real earnings per worker. Preliminary data for 1988 and 1989 support the expectation of future improvements in productivity and earnings:

	Output per Hour	GNP per Worker	Earnings per Worker
1969-79	1.3%	0.4%	0.1%
1979-84	1.1	0.6	0.8
1984-87	1.6	1.0	1.5
1987-89 preliminary	n.a.	1.6	1.8

This expectation is represented in the baseline projection, which depicts the U.S. economy paralleling its 1955-65 business cycle experience (Chart 17). However, deep recessions could set back the process of capital formation and productivity growth. If the recession pattern of the 1980s were repeated in future decades, overall economic growth between 1989 and 2010 would be reduced by 0.4 percent per year, and GNP would follow the time path indicated by the severe cycles projection shown in Chart 17.

Chart 17

GNP under Different Business Cycle Projections, 1980-2010

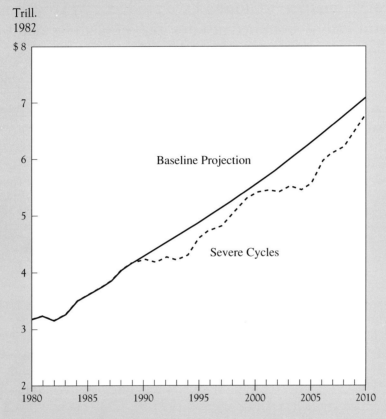

Trill.
1982

Baseline Projection

Severe Cycles

Note: The baseline projection is consistent with moderate cyclical fluctuations. It is based on the average unemployment levels experienced during the years 1955-1965. The severe business cycles' projection is derived by assuming the unemployment rates of the years 1979-1988 will be repeated in each future decade.

Sources: 1980-1988 (Actual): BEA. 1989-2010 (Predicted): NPA Data Services, Inc.

Although U.S. productivity levels remain the highest worldwide, other industrial nations are approaching these levels. The critical question for future U.S. productivity growth is whether it can be sustained at rates high enough to maintain growth in real per capita income.

The absolute levels of productivity as measured by the gross domestic product per person employed have remained higher in the United States than in other major industrial countries since 1950 (Chart 18). However, because productivity increases have been generally lower in the United States, these countries have been approaching the U.S. levels. By 1988, Canadian productivity was within 5 percent of the U.S. level; German (and also French and Italian) productivity within 15 percent; and Japanese and U.K. productivity within 25 percent.

Past productivity gains for other nations may have been greater than U.S. gains because of the higher existing U.S. levels. Now, however, the gap between the U.S. levels and those of the other countries has diminished substantially. Furthermore, in a number of industries, productivity levels are already higher abroad than in the U.S., creating new opportunities for the United States to utilize foreign productivity experience.

Productivity growth rates in the range of 1.2 to 1.5 percent a year are needed to support stable growth in U.S. per capita income and are well within the range of past experience in the U.S. and other industrial nations. The average U.S. productivity growth rate over the period 1950-88 was 1.4 percent a year. In the period 1979-88, GDP per employed person in the major European countries grew between 1.5 and 2.0 percent annually—as their productivity levels began to approach those of the United States—while the U.S. growth averaged 1.0 percent.

Chart 18

Productivity in Selected Major Industrial Countries, 1950-1988
(GDP per Person Employed)

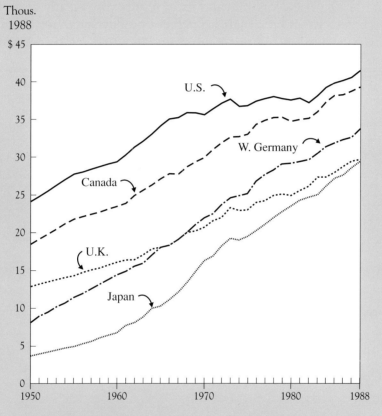

Note: Productivity is measured by the gross domestic product converted into U.S. dollars by the OECD purchasing power parity exchange rates.

Source: Office of Productivity and Technology, BLS (August 1989). Based on data compiled by the Organization for Economic Cooperation and Development.

The key variable for economic expansion is productivity growth. Likely differences in future productivity growth have much more serious implications for the economy than do likely future demographic variations.

Because there has been at least some productivity growth in most historical periods, a reasonable minimum future annual growth rate in productivity (output per hour in the private business sector) is projected to be 0.8 percent, corresponding to the recent period of slow growth. A top rate is assumed to be 1.8 percent. Future productivity growth is not likely to reach rates greater than the 2.0 percent that prevailed in the 1950s and 1960s. The economic and fiscal results vary greatly between the low 0.8 percent and the high 1.8 percent productivity growth projections, as is shown in the following tables and in Chart 19. By comparison, the effects on U.S. economic growth of alternate assumptions about immigration or retirement are small.

	GNP per Capita	Population	Persons Employed	GNP per Person Employed	GNP
1950-1969	2.2%	1.5%	1.6%	2.2%	3.8%
1969-1979	1.7	1.1	2.2	0.6	2.8
1979-1984	0.8	1.0	1.2	0.6	1.9
1984-1989 (prelim.)	2.5	1.0	2.3	1.2	3.5

Baseline Projection: Productivity Growth at 1.3%

1989-2000	1.8	0.8	1.4	1.2	2.6
2000-2010	1.8	0.6	1.1	1.3	2.4

High Projection: Productivity Growth at 1.8%

1989-2000	2.3	0.8	1.5	1.6	3.1
2000-2010	2.2	0.6	1.2	1.6	2.8

Low Projection: Productivity Growth at 0.8%

1989-2000	1.4	0.8	1.4	0.8	2.2
2000-2010	1.2	0.6	1.0	0.8	1.8

The baseline (1.3 percent) projection indicates per capita GNP growth comparable to that of the past two decades. The high (1.8 percent) projection would permit expansion at the rates of the 1950s and 1960s, and the low (0.8 percent) projection—if sustainable—would permit per capita growth of 1.2 to 1.4 percent. However, in view of the size of the U.S. trade and budget deficits that this low productivity growth implies, the projection may not be supportable.

Chart 19

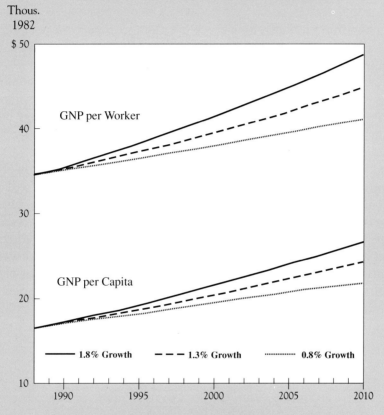

Impact of Productivity Assumptions on GNP
per Worker and GNP per Capita, 1988-2010

Thous.
1982
$ 50

GNP per Worker

40

30

GNP per Capita

20

——— 1.8% Growth   - - - 1.3% Growth   ·············· 0.8% Growth

10
1990   1995   2000   2005   2010

Sources: 1988 (Actual): BEA and BLS. 1989-2010 (Predicted): NPA Data
Services, Inc.

Future productivity growth will determine whether net fixed capital formation grows or stagnates.

The baseline productivity growth averaging 1.3 percent per year would permit future growth in net capital investment and increases in the capital-labor ratio.

Productivity growth of 1.8 percent would support substantial annual additions to the U.S. stock of fixed capital net of depreciation (Chart 20). These capital additions would accelerate the growth in the capital-labor ratio from 1.3 percent a year in 1979-1989 to 1.9 percent in 1989-2000 and to 2.3 percent in 2000-2010.

Productivity growth of 0.8 percent implies a constant and lower growth rate in the capital-labor ratio of 1.4 percent. This would still support continued growth in productivity and per capita income. However, this outcome assumes that the funds for capital investment will be forthcoming during the entire period to 2010 in spite of the large U.S. trade and budget deficits implied by the low growth. Because an indefinite continuation of the deficits projected with low productivity is not plausible, maintenance of investment and growth implied by the 0.8 percent productivity growth may not be possible.

Chart 20

Impact of Productivity Assumptions on Net Fixed Nonresidential Investment, 1988-2010

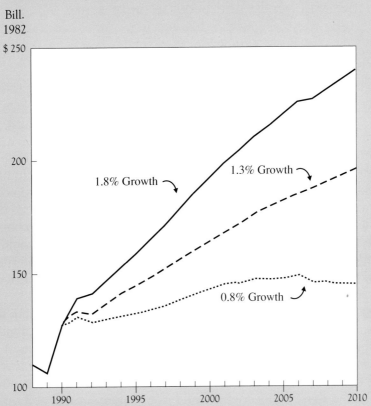

Bill. 1982

Sources: 1988 (Actual): BEA. 1989-2010 (Predicted): NPA Data Services, Inc.

With higher productivity growth, federal deficit problems could be solved within 10 years. With low productivity growth, they will persist and become more acute.

Radically different federal surplus/deficit projections result from the alternate productivity increases (Chart 21).

The baseline projection assumes for the federal government constant real defense expenditure, 2 percent growth in real medicare outlays per person 65 and older, 1 percent growth in average real social security benefits, a 6 percent ratio of net interest paid to outside debt, 3 percent real growth in social insurance contributions, gradual decline in the corporate income tax over the next 10 years, and an otherwise unchanged tax and expenditure system in relation to the economy. This projection forecasts a decline in the budget deficit to a level near balance. (If there were moderate cuts in defense spending, the budget would be in balance.)

At 1.8 percent growth in productivity, the federal deficit could be eliminated in less than 10 years, and subsequent growth would permit substantial tax reductions, spending increases, funding of social security reserves, or debt retirement.

However, at 0.8 percent productivity growth, the federal deficit would deepen progressively from about $100 billion (in 1982 dollars) to nearly $300 billion a year by 2010. Even with the moderate interest rate assumption, the cumulative deficits that would be added to the debt with no means available for reducing the real load of indebtedness would create a fiscal crisis. Such a course could not be maintained, and serious monetary and social crises would be likely well before the end of the projection period. These crises would most probably involve financial instability, severe cuts in public programs (or declines in their real value through inflation), increased real tax loads, and other hardships. It is extremely unlikely that the continued increases in real per capita consumption requiring escalating real amounts of government borrowing could be maintained.

Chart 21

Impact of Productivity Assumptions on
Federal Surplus/Deficit Projections, 1988-2010

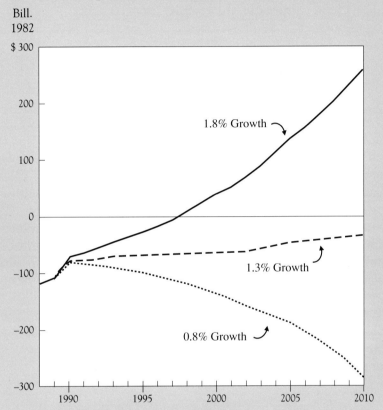

Bill.
1982

Sources: 1988 (Actual): BEA. 1989-2010 (Predicted): NPA Data
Services, Inc.

With low productivity, net foreign investment deficits are likely to grow, but higher productivity would permit their elimination in a relatively short time.

In the baseline projection, the U.S. savings-investment balance implies that the net foreign investment deficit could decline and turn to surplus by 2000 (Chart 22). With the high projection, it could turn positive before 1995. But with the low projection, the shortfall would grow and may become insupportable.

Growth in per capita GNP and income, projected here even with modest growth in productivity for the period 1989-2010 (Chart 19), is unstable and could be undermined by several unfavorable developments. As indicated, severe recessions and/or a runaway federal deficit could seriously hurt the prospect for continued increases in U.S. economic well-being. Another threat to long-term U.S. growth is the possibility of a persistent foreign account deficit, especially if combined with ongoing government deficits and a stagnating economy.

Increasing foreign indebtedness could adversely affect the U.S. standard of living by driving up interest rates, reducing the purchasing power of U.S. dollars for foreign goods, and generating a net outflow of income in interest and profit payments with depressing effects on domestic investment.

Chart 22

Impact of Productivity Assumptions on U.S. Net Foreign Investment, 1988-2010

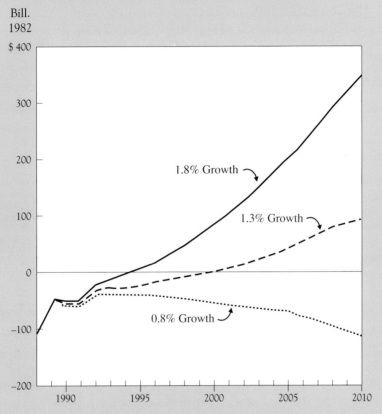

Bill.
1982

Note: U.S. net foreign investment was calculated as a residual from the gross savings-fixed investment balance in the National Income and Product Accounts. The net foreign investment series projected here assumes that the relatively minor items of net change in business inventories and statistical discrepancy equal zero.

Sources: 1988 (Actual): BEA. 1989-2010 (Predicted): NPA Data Services, Inc.

Technical Note

Most of the economic data were obtained from the National Income and Product Accounts (NIPA) database of the Bureau of Economic Analysis, U.S. Department of Commerce.

NPA Data Services, Inc., projections were prepared in August 1989 following the July 1989 update of the NIPA data. These projections were derived through an econometric growth model of the United States in which labor force participation rates, income, employment, productivity, and other variables are estimated simultaneously in a mutually dependent fashion. A set of assumptions was used about future population, government activity and other independent variables. In this model, productivity is defined as the output per hour in the private business sector. All variables are expressed in real terms. The data series for which no price deflators are provided is converted to constant dollars by using the national income deflator as an approximate price series.

These projections differ somewhat from other projections because they incorporate more current data and use a somewhat different estimating methodology. For example, the growth model used in the NPA Data Services projections allows for participation rates of women to depend on the number of children and on the college education of women of different ages. The participation rates of older workers depend on relative levels of retirement income and earnings of workers. Other models do not incorporate these factors.

The population assumption differs from the constant assumption of a decline in immigration from its present level to a constant immigration flow of 500,000 by the end of the century—made by the Census Bureau middle series projection—in that a constant rate of immigration as of a recent date (1985) is applied to future population estimates. This assumption was made because an increase in future immigration appears to be more realistic, and is supported by the latest available data.

The calculations of the effects of different rates of productivity growth on the economy include both the direct effects of changes in productivity growth on GNP and the indirect effects on labor force participation and other variables. The projections assume that except for a future cut in the corporate income tax to an average rate of 25 percent, the tax system will remain unchanged at all levels of government (but the tax base and the revenues may change); the ratio of government interest payments to federal debt held by the public is constant (frozen at 6 percent in 1990); defense spending remains constant at the 1988 level; real social security and medicare payments per beneficiary grow at a moderate rate reflecting recent changes; the personal savings rate remains frozen at 5 percent of disposable personal income; and retained earnings are frozen at 35 percent of adjusted corporate profits after tax from 1990 on.

The gross savings-investment equation is used to derive the residual that implies the level of net foreign investment. Gross savings consist of: personal savings; undistributed corporate profits; corporate and noncorporate capital consumption allowance; and total (federal, state and local) government surplus (negative if deficit). Gross investment consists of: gross fixed private (residential and nonresidential) investment; and net foreign investment. In the equation, gross savings are equal to gross investment. (Net change in business inventories and statistical discrepancy in future years are implicitly assumed to be zero.)

Statistical Tables for the Baseline Projection

STATISTICAL TABLE 1

UNITED STATES POPULATION SUMMARIES AS OF JULY 1
(Thousands)

Year	U.S. Population Total Incl. Armed forces	Resident	Civilian	Armed Forces Total	Resident	Overseas
1950	152,271	151,868	150,790	1,481	1,078	403
...	...	...	...	...	...	...
1960	180,671	179,979	178,140	2,531	1,839	692
...	...	...	...	...	...	...
1965	194,303	193,526	191,605	2,698	1,921	777
1966	196,560	195,576	193,420	3,140	2,156	984
1967	198,712	197,457	195,264	3,448	2,193	1,255
1968	200,706	199,399	197,113	3,593	2,286	1,307
1969	202,677	201,385	199,145	3,532	2,240	1,292
1970	205,052	203,984	201,895	3,157	2,089	1,068
1971	207,661	206,827	204,866	2,795	1,961	834
1972	209,896	209,284	207,511	2,385	1,773	612
1973	211,909	211,357	209,600	2,309	1,757	552
1974	213,854	213,342	211,636	2,218	1,706	512
1975	215,973	215,465	213,788	2,185	1,677	508
1976	218,035	217,563	215,894	2,141	1,669	472
1977	220,239	219,760	218,106	2,133	1,654	479
1978	222,585	222,095	220,467	2,118	1,628	490
1979	225,055	224,567	222,969	2,086	1,598	488
1980	227,757	227,255	225,651	2,106	1,604	502
1981	230,138	229,637	227,989	2,149	1,648	501
1982	232,520	231,996	230,327	2,193	1,669	524
1983	234,799	234,284	232,589	2,210	1,695	515
1984	237,001	236,477	234,762	2,239	1,715	524
1985	239,279	238,736	237,031	2,248	1,705	543
1986	241,625	241,107	239,386	2,239	1,721	518
1987	243,934	243,419	241,680	2,254	1,739	515
1988	246,329	245,807	244,125	2,204	1,682	522
1989	248,857	248,337	246,444	2,204	1,685	519
1990	250,914	250,395	248,710	2,204	1,685	519
1991	253,150	252,631	250,946	2,204	1,685	519
1992	255,331	254,812	253,127	2,204	1,685	519
1993	257,453	256,934	255,249	2,204	1,685	519
1994	259,516	258,997	257,312	2,204	1,685	519
1995	261,544	261,025	259,340	2,204	1,685	519
1996	263,508	262,989	261,304	2,204	1,685	519
1997	265,409	264,890	263,205	2,204	1,685	519
1998	267,270	266,751	265,066	2,204	1,685	519
1999	269,091	268,572	266,887	2,204	1,685	519
2000	270,898	270,379	268,694	2,204	1,685	519
2001	272,662	272,143	270,458	2,204	1,685	519
2002	274,410	273,891	272,206	2,204	1,685	519
2003	276,115	275,596	273,911	2,204	1,685	519
2004	277,831	277,312	275,627	2,204	1,685	519
2005	279,557	279,038	277,353	2,204	1,685	519
2006	281,266	280,747	279,062	2,204	1,685	519
2007	282,957	282,438	280,753	2,204	1,685	519
2008	284,630	284,111	282,426	2,204	1,685	519
2009	286,285	285,766	284,081	2,204	1,685	519
2010	287,949	287,430	285,745	2,204	1,685	519

Sources: U.S. Bureau of the Census and NPA Data Services, Inc.

STATISTICAL TABLE 2

COMPONENTS OF U.S. POPULATION CHANGE, CALENDAR YEARS
(Thousands)

Year	Total Population as of Jan. 1	Births	Deaths	Natural Increase	Net Civilian Immigration	Net Change
1950	151,135	3,645	1,468	2,177	299	2,476
1951	153,622	3,845	1,501	2,344	335	2,679
1952	156,309	3,933	1,512	2,421	242	2,663
1953	158,973	3,989	1,531	2,458	261	2,719
1954	161,690	4,102	1,489	2,613	287	2,900
1955	164,588	4,128	1,537	2,591	337	2,928
1956	167,513	4,244	1,572	2,672	387	3,059
1957	170,571	4,332	1,641	2,691	272	2,963
1958	173,533	4,279	1,655	2,624	292	2,916
1959	176,447	4,313	1,663	2,650	292	2,942
1960	179,386	4,307	1,708	2,599	327	2,926
1961	182,287	4,317	1,703	2,614	373	2,987
1962	185,242	4,213	1,758	2,455	351	2,806
1963	188,013	4,142	1,815	2,327	361	2,688
1964	190,668	4,070	1,799	2,271	317	2,588
1965	193,223	3,801	1,830	1,971	373	2,344
1966	194,551	3,642	1,869	1,773	455	1,328
1967	197,636	3,555	1,861	1,694	414	3,085
1968	199,709	3,535	1,948	1,587	398	2,073
1969	201,692	3,630	1,934	1,696	453	1,983
1970	203,849	3,739	1,927	1,812	438	2,158
1971	206,466	3,556	1,930	1,626	387	2,617
1972	208,917	3,258	1,965	1,293	325	2,451
1973	210,985	3,137	1,974	1,163	331	2,068
1974	212,932	3,160	1,935	1,225	316	1,947
1975	214,931	3,144	1,894	1,250	449	1,999
1976	217,095	3,168	1,910	1,258	353	2,164
1977	219,179	3,327	1,900	1,427	394	2,084
1978	221,477	3,333	1,928	1,405	508	2,298
1979	223,865	3,494	1,914	1,580	540	2,388
1980	226,451	3,612	1,990	1,622	845	2,586
1981	229,033	3,629	1,979	1,650	718	2,582
1982	231,405	3,681	1,975	1,706	626	2,372
1983	233,736	3,639	2,020	1,619	605	2,331
1984	235,961	3,669	2,040	1,629	615	2,225
1985	238,207	3,750	2,083	1,667	648	2,246
1986	240,552	3,687	2,093	1,594	654	2,345
1987	242,843	3,819	2,161	1,658	661	2,280
1988	245,231	3,829	2,181	1,648	667	2,329
1989	247,635	3,755	2,163	1,591	675	2,266
1990	249,663	3,739	2,183	1,556	681	2,236
1991	251,844	3,696	2,202	1,494	687	2,180
1992	253,966	3,651	2,221	1,430	693	2,123
1993	256,029	3,604	2,240	1,365	698	2,063
1994	258,057	3,581	2,258	1,324	704	2,028
1995	260,021	3,531	2,275	1,255	710	1,965
1996	261,922	3,505	2,319	1,186	715	1,901
1997	263,783	3,477	2,336	1,141	720	1,861
1998	265,604	3,448	2,352	1,096	725	1,821
1999	267,411	3,444	2,368	1,076	730	1,806
2000	269,175	3,413	2,384	1,029	735	1,764
2001	270,923	3,408	2,399	1,009	740	1,749
2002	272,628	3,403	2,442	960	744	1,705
2003	274,344	3,424	2,457	966	749	1,715
2004	276,070	3,445	2,473	972	754	1,726
2005	277,779	3,439	2,488	950	758	1,709
2006	279,470	3,460	2,531	928	763	1,691
2007	281,143	3,480	2,575	905	768	1,673
2008	282,798	3,501	2,619	882	772	1,655
2009	284,462	3,521	2,634	887	777	1,664
2010	286,107	3,542	2,678	864	781	1,645

Sources: U.S. Bureau of the Census and NPA Data Services, Inc.

LABOR FORCE AND EMPLOYMENT
(Thousands)

Year	Total Labor Force	Total Employed	Civilian Labor Force		
			Total	Male	Female
1950	63,855	60,567	62,206	43,817	18,389
1951	65,126	63,059	62,028	43,005	19,024
1952	65,708	63,843	62,115	42,870	19,245
1953	66,561	64,726	63,014	43,634	19,380
1954	66,992	63,459	63,642	43,965	19,677
1955	68,070	65,218	65,022	44,473	20,549
1956	69,410	66,655	66,554	45,093	21,461
1957	69,709	66,870	66,910	45,178	21,732
1958	70,272	65,672	67,636	45,518	22,118
1959	70,920	67,181	68,369	45,885	22,484
1960	72,141	68,292	69,627	46,389	23,238
1961	73,035	68,318	70,463	46,656	23,807
1962	73,444	69,529	70,617	46,600	24,017
1963	74,569	70,499	71,832	47,127	24,706
1964	75,820	72,043	73,082	47,676	25,406
1965	77,175	73,810	74,453	48,251	26,202
1966	78,900	76,017	75,778	48,474	27,304
1967	80,794	77,818	77,348	48,986	28,362
1968	82,190	79,454	78,656	49,451	29,205
1969	84,242	81,408	80,736	50,222	30,514
1970	85,963	81,866	82,775	51,233	31,542
1971	87,194	82,183	84,378	52,176	32,202
1972	89,483	84,602	87,034	53,554	33,480
1973	92,086	87,390	89,760	54,624	35,136
1974	94,515	89,023	92,286	55,742	36,543
1975	95,951	88,026	93,771	56,295	37,476
1976	98,302	90,896	96,158	57,174	38,983
1977	101,142	94,150	99,009	58,396	40,613
1978	104,368	98,165	102,251	59,620	42,613
1979	107,050	100,912	104,962	60,726	44,235
1980	109,042	101,405	106,940	61,453	45,487
1981	110,812	102,539	108,670	61,947	46,696
1982	112,383	101,705	110,204	62,450	47,755
1983	113,749	103,033	111,550	63,047	48,503
1984	115,763	107,224	113,544	63,835	49,709
1985	117,695	109,384	115,461	64,411	51,050
1986	120,078	111,841	117,834	65,422	52,413
1987	122,122	114,697	119,865	66,207	53,658
1988	123,893	117,192	121,669	66,927	54,742
1989	126,475	119,889	124,251	68,020	56,231
1990	128,696	122,119	126,472	69,023	57,449
1991	130,465	123,796	128,241	69,718	58,523
1992	132,307	125,543	130,083	70,475	59,608
1993	134,147	127,287	131,923	71,254	60,668
1994	135,969	129,015	133,745	72,042	61,704
1995	137,805	130,755	135,581	72,840	62,741
1996	139,682	132,534	137,458	73,709	63,749
1997	141,720	134,467	139,496	74,618	64,879
1998	143,754	136,395	141,530	75,539	65,991
1999	145,754	138,291	143,530	76,463	67,067
2000	147,736	140,169	145,512	77,392	68,120
2001	149,585	141,922	147,361	78,274	69,087
2002	151,454	143,694	149,230	79,168	70,063
2003	153,253	145,399	151,029	80,048	70,981
2004	155,044	147,097	152,820	80,933	71,887
2005	156,941	148,896	154,717	81,842	72,876
2006	158,407	150,286	156,183	82,587	73,596
2007	160,020	151,815	157,796	83,343	74,453
2008	161,611	153,323	159,387	84,103	75,285
2009	163,164	154,795	160,940	84,859	76,081
2010	164,700	156,251	162,476	85,616	76,860

Sources: BLS and NPA Data Services, Inc.

STATISTICAL TABLE 4

CHANGES IN CIVILIAN LABOR FORCE
(Thousands)

Year	Total	Under 25	Female 25+	Male 25+
1950	910	-108	687	332
1951	-178	-824	604	43
1952	87	-788	378	497
1953	899	-400	260	1040
1954	628	-53	322	359
1955	1380	307	810	263
1956	1532	474	764	294
1957	356	110	285	-39
1958	726	189	356	181
1959	733	374	327	31
1960	1257	635	494	128
1961	836	348	359	129
1962	154	109	102	-57
1963	1216	608	449	159
1964	1250	745	363	142
1965	1371	814	446	110
1966	1326	797	516	13
1967	1570	572	664	334
1968	1309	302	529	478
1969	2080	1018	779	283
1970	2038	995	602	441
1971	1603	951	395	257
1972	2656	1380	728	548
1973	2726	1166	1122	439
1974	2526	841	947	738
1975	1486	432	620	434
1976	2387	724	1172	490
1977	2851	834	1196	821
1978	3242	865	1471	906
1979	2711	363	1405	943
1980	1978	-107	1324	761
1981	1730	-185	1237	678
1982	1534	-516	1198	853
1983	1346	-375	954	767
1984	1994	-240	1272	963
1985	1917	-367	1396	888
1986	2373	-245	1443	1175
1987	2031	-373	1330	1074
1988	1804	-469	1337	936
1989	2582	-305	1569	1317
1990	2221	-71	1230	1062
1991	1769	57	1043	669
1992	1843	21	1074	748
1993	1839	4	1061	774
1994	1823	-11	1046	788
1995	1835	-22	1055	802
1996	1877	299	861	717
1997	2039	267	998	774
1998	2034	263	984	787
1999	2000	259	950	791
2000	1981	257	928	796
2001	1850	374	793	683
2002	1869	338	817	715
2003	1799	332	761	705
2004	1791	332	750	709
2005	1897	332	831	734
2006	1466	164	643	660
2007	1613	135	791	687
2008	1591	131	766	695
2009	1552	127	732	693
2010	1536	126	714	696

Sources: BLS and NPA Data Services, Inc.

STATISTICAL TABLE 5

GNP AND EARNINGS
(Monetary Amounts in 1982 $)

Year	GNP (Bill.)	GNP per Person Employed	GNP per Capita	Ratio of Earnings to GNP	Earnings per Person Employed
1950	$ 1204	$ 19872	$ 7904	0.547	$ 10872
1951	1328	21064	8576	0.567	11950
1952	1380	21616	8759	0.571	12348
1953	1435	22175	8960	0.579	12848
1954	1416	22317	8687	0.571	12740
1955	1495	22922	9009	0.562	12876
1956	1526	22890	9033	0.579	13253
1957	1551	23197	9019	0.579	13433
1958	1539	23439	8802	0.574	13456
1959	1629	24249	9161	0.573	13906
1960	1665	24385	9217	0.582	14198
1961	1709	25011	9302	0.579	14476
1962	1800	25881	9647	0.576	14901
1963	1873	26572	9899	0.576	15315
1964	1973	27389	10283	0.577	15797
1965	2088	28283	10744	0.572	16169
1966	2208	29051	11235	0.575	16698
1967	2271	29186	11430	0.586	17116
1968	2366	29773	11786	0.591	17610
1969	2423	29766	11956	0.604	17987
1970	2416	29514	11783	0.611	18025
1971	2485	30236	11966	0.600	18153
1972	2609	30834	12428	0.599	18460
1973	2744	31399	12949	0.595	18676
1974	2729	30658	12762	0.605	18541
1975	2694	30608	12475	0.594	18175
1976	2827	31098	12964	0.592	18415
1977	2958	31421	13432	0.588	18487
1978	3115	31734	13996	0.586	18600
1979	3192	31634	14185	0.589	18637
1980	3187	31430	13994	0.598	18785
1981	3249	31684	14117	0.594	18832
1982	3166	31129	13616	0.602	18750
1983	3279	31826	13966	0.596	18976
1984	3501	32655	14774	0.595	19445
1985	3619	33083	15123	0.599	19815
1986	3718	33243	15389	0.602	20012
1987	3854	33599	15794	0.605	20324
1988	4024	34340	16338	0.602	20680
1989	4161	34710	16736	0.607	21078
1990	4282	35062	17064	0.609	21343
1991	4384	35410	17316	0.610	21613
1992	4498	35831	17618	0.612	21929
1993	4619	36287	17941	0.614	22268
1994	4738	36725	18257	0.613	22523
1995	4860	37166	18580	0.613	22780
1996	4986	37618	18920	0.613	23045
1997	5115	38040	19273	0.612	23291
1998	5247	38469	19632	0.612	23541
1999	5381	38912	19997	0.612	23799
2000	5518	39368	20370	0.611	24066
2001	5658	39864	20750	0.611	24360
2002	5800	40365	21137	0.611	24658
2003	5946	40894	21534	0.611	24971
2004	6094	41431	21936	0.610	25291
2005	6246	41947	22341	0.610	25596
2006	6396	42558	22740	0.610	25962
2007	6549	43136	23144	0.610	26307
2008	6704	43727	23554	0.610	26660
2009	6861	44326	23967	0.610	27018
2010	7020	44929	24380	0.609	27378

Sources: BLS, BEA and NPA Data Services, Inc.

STATISTICAL TABLE 6

FIXED NONRESIDENTIAL INVESTMENT AND CAPITAL
(1982 $)

| Year | Fixed Investment (Bill.) | | Net Capital Stock | |
	Gross	Net	Total (Bill.)	Per Worker (Thous.)
1950	124.0	43.3	1023	16.9
1951	131.7	46.9	1069	17.0
1952	130.6	41.6	1110	17.4
1953	140.0	47.0	1156	17.9
1954	137.6	40.4	1196	18.8
1955	151.1	50.0	1244	19.1
1956	160.4	54.9	1299	19.5
1957	161.1	51.7	1350	20.2
1958	143.9	31.5	1379	21.0
1959	153.6	38.5	1417	21.1
1960	159.4	41.4	1458	21.3
1961	158.2	37.3	1495	21.9
1962	170.2	46.4	1541	22.2
1963	176.7	49.3	1590	22.6
1964	194.9	63.2	1653	22.9
1965	227.6	90.4	1742	23.6
1966	250.4	106.2	1842	24.2
1967	245.0	93.6	1932	24.8
1968	254.5	96.0	2024	25.5
1969	269.7	103.1	2125	26.1
1970	264.0	89.3	2212	27.0
1971	258.3	76.1	2286	27.8
1972	277.0	85.3	2370	28.0
1973	317.3	116.5	2486	28.4
1974	317.9	106.9	2593	29.1
1975	281.2	60.8	2655	30.2
1976	290.6	61.8	2714	29.9
1977	324.0	85.1	2799	29.7
1978	362.1	111.5	2909	29.6
1979	389.4	124.3	3033	30.1
1980	379.2	101.4	3138	30.9
1981	395.2	105.5	3244	31.6
1982	366.7	65.5	3307	32.5
1983	361.1	50.3	3357	32.6
1984	425.2	103.3	3456	32.2
1985	453.5	116.1	3577	32.7
1986	438.4	85.7	3670	32.8
1987	455.5	88.1	3760	32.8
1988	493.8	110.0	3869	33.0
1989	508.8	106.0	3975	33.2
1990	528.3	126.8	4102	33.6
1991	547.5	133.2	4235	34.2
1992	559.9	132.2	4367	34.8
1993	578.0	136.9	4504	35.4
1994	596.2	141.3	4645	36.0
1995	613.6	144.4	4790	36.6
1996	631.8	148.0	4938	37.3
1997	650.8	152.0	5090	37.9
1998	670.2	156.1	5246	38.5
1999	689.9	160.1	5406	39.1
2000	710.1	164.1	5570	39.7
2001	730.7	168.1	5738	40.4
2002	751.5	171.9	5910	41.1
2003	772.9	176.0	6086	41.9
2004	793.6	178.9	6265	42.6
2005	814.8	182.0	6447	43.3
2006	836.3	185.2	6632	44.1
2007	857.2	187.4	6820	44.9
2008	878.9	190.1	7010	45.7
2009	901.0	193.0	7203	46.5
2010	923.2	195.7	7399	47.4

Sources: BEA and NPA Data Services, Inc.

STATISTICAL TABLE 7

PERCENTAGE CHANGE FROM PREVIOUS YEAR

Year	Total Population	Total Persons Employed	GNP	GNP per Person Employed	GNP per Capita	Total Earnings
1950	2.1	2.2	8.5	6.2	6.3	4.8
1951	1.7	4.1	10.4	6.0	8.5	9.9
1952	1.7	1.2	3.9	2.6	2.1	3.3
1953	1.7	1.4	4.0	2.6	2.3	4.0
1954	1.8	-2.0	-1.3	0.6	-3.1	-0.8
1955	1.8	2.8	5.6	2.7	3.7	1.1
1956	1.8	2.2	2.1	-0.1	0.3	2.9
1957	1.8	0.3	1.7	1.3	-0.2	1.4
1958	1.7	-1.8	-0.8	1.0	-2.4	0.2
1959	1.7	2.3	5.8	3.5	4.1	3.3
1960	1.6	1.7	2.2	0.6	0.6	2.1
1961	1.7	0.0	2.6	2.6	0.9	2.0
1962	1.5	1.8	5.3	3.5	3.7	2.9
1963	1.4	1.4	4.1	2.7	2.6	2.8
1964	1.4	2.2	5.3	3.1	3.9	3.1
1965	1.3	2.5	5.8	3.3	4.5	2.4
1966	1.2	3.0	5.8	2.7	4.6	3.3
1967	1.1	2.4	2.8	0.5	1.7	2.5
1968	1.0	2.1	4.2	2.0	3.1	2.9
1969	1.0	2.5	2.4	-0.0	1.4	2.1
1970	1.2	0.6	-0.3	-0.8	-1.4	0.2
1971	1.3	0.4	2.8	2.4	1.6	0.7
1972	1.1	2.9	5.0	2.0	3.9	1.7
1973	1.0	3.3	5.2	1.8	4.2	1.2
1974	0.9	1.9	-0.5	-2.4	-1.4	-0.7
1975	1.0	-1.1	-1.3	-0.2	-2.3	-2.0
1976	1.0	3.3	4.9	1.6	3.9	1.3
1977	1.0	3.6	4.7	1.0	3.6	0.4
1978	1.1	4.3	5.3	1.0	4.2	0.6
1979	1.1	2.8	2.5	-0.3	1.4	0.2
1980	1.2	0.5	-0.2	-0.6	-1.3	0.8
1981	1.0	1.1	1.9	0.8	0.9	0.2
1982	1.0	-0.8	-2.5	-1.7	-3.5	-0.4
1983	1.0	1.3	3.6	2.2	2.6	1.2
1984	0.9	4.1	6.8	2.6	5.8	2.5
1985	1.0	2.0	3.4	1.3	2.4	1.9
1986	1.0	2.2	2.7	0.5	1.8	1.0
1987	1.0	2.6	3.7	1.1	2.6	1.6
1988	1.0	2.2	4.4	2.2	3.4	1.7
1989	0.9	2.3	3.4	1.1	2.4	1.9
1990	0.9	1.9	2.9	1.0	2.0	1.3
1991	0.9	1.4	2.4	1.0	1.5	1.3
1992	0.9	1.4	2.6	1.2	1.7	1.5
1993	0.8	1.4	2.7	1.3	1.8	1.5
1994	0.8	1.4	2.6	1.2	1.8	1.1
1995	0.8	1.3	2.6	1.2	1.8	1.1
1996	0.8	1.4	2.6	1.2	1.8	1.2
1997	0.7	1.5	2.6	1.1	1.9	1.1
1998	0.7	1.4	2.6	1.1	1.9	1.1
1999	0.7	1.4	2.6	1.2	1.9	1.1
2000	0.7	1.4	2.5	1.2	1.9	1.1
2001	0.7	1.3	2.5	1.3	1.9	1.2
2002	0.6	1.2	2.5	1.3	1.9	1.2
2003	0.6	1.2	2.5	1.3	1.9	1.3
2004	0.6	1.2	2.5	1.3	1.9	1.3
2005	0.6	1.2	2.5	1.2	1.9	1.2
2006	0.6	0.9	2.4	1.5	1.8	1.4
2007	0.6	1.0	2.4	1.4	1.8	1.3
2008	0.6	1.0	2.4	1.4	1.8	1.3
2009	0.6	1.0	2.3	1.4	1.8	1.3
2010	0.6	0.9	2.3	1.4	1.7	1.3

Source: NPA Data Services, Inc.

STATISTICAL TABLE 8

GROSS SAVINGS
(Bill. 1982 $)

Year	Gross Savings	Personal Savings	Undistributed Corporate Profits	Capital Consumption Allowance	Federal Surplus (Deficit)	State and Local Surplus (Deficit)
1950	223.9	53.4	25.1	106.5	39.0	(5.1)
1951	229.8	67.2	24.5	111.8	26.3	(1.6)
1952	197.5	69.9	25.4	117.0	(14.9)	0.0
1953	190.8	72.7	24.1	122.1	(28.1)	0.4
1954	193.1	63.3	25.5	127.4	(23.2)	(4.2)
1955	241.0	59.5	32.5	132.6	16.4	(4.8)
1956	267.3	76.9	30.1	138.3	22.0	(3.2)
1957	259.8	79.1	29.1	143.5	8.0	(4.9)
1958	220.7	82.7	25.4	147.7	(35.0)	(8.2)
1959	252.9	72.4	32.2	151.9	(3.7)	(1.3)
1960	264.8	68.0	30.8	156.3	9.8	0.3
1961	259.7	80.6	31.1	160.6	(12.6)	(1.3)
1962	271.8	82.0	38.0	165.1	(13.3)	1.6
1963	288.9	76.9	40.8	170.3	0.9	1.6
1964	308.8	96.6	46.0	176.3	(10.1)	3.1
1965	340.2	102.4	52.7	183.7	1.5	0.0
1966	343.3	103.2	53.2	192.2	(5.2)	1.4
1967	340.9	126.3	50.5	201.1	(37.0)	(3.1)
1968	355.0	113.3	47.9	209.8	(16.0)	0.3
1969	390.2	106.8	42.3	219.8	21.3	3.8
1970	371.7	137.7	33.7	229.8	(29.6)	4.3
1971	378.8	150.0	39.0	239.5	(49.8)	5.9
1972	393.6	132.0	44.3	253.4	(36.1)	29.0
1973	476.0	178.7	45.0	263.6	(11.2)	27.1
1974	466.0	179.1	32.3	276.1	(21.5)	13.3
1975	385.7	176.4	39.4	287.0	(117.0)	7.6
1976	409.1	151.6	44.9	297.3	(84.7)	24.1
1977	428.4	134.2	52.7	309.6	(68.0)	39.8
1978	489.5	151.4	54.7	323.7	(40.2)	39.7
1979	519.4	148.9	49.5	341.3	(20.3)	34.8
1980	481.6	159.2	37.6	356.1	(71.3)	31.2
1981	511.8	170.3	40.0	369.7	(68.2)	36.4
1982	421.7	153.9	30.5	383.2	(145.9)	35.1
1983	398.7	125.1	45.8	394.4	(166.5)	45.5
1984	456.2	151.7	56.0	407.2	(158.6)	59.7
1985	417.9	112.4	58.3	426.7	(179.4)	58.3
1986	423.3	108.5	53.4	443.4	(182.0)	53.2
1987	465.6	85.5	55.0	460.8	(135.7)	44.5
1988	533.2	117.5	53.9	480.2	(118.4)	44.7
1989	612.6	172.5	46.5	501.7	(108.1)	41.0
1990	645.0	153.8	50.4	519.3	(78.5)	25.0
1991	669.1	157.7	52.5	537.1	(78.1)	25.0
1992	696.8	162.0	54.7	555.2	(75.0)	25.0
1993	726.7	166.4	57.1	573.5	(70.4)	25.0
1994	753.5	170.5	59.5	592.2	(68.8)	25.0
1995	781.1	174.7	62.0	611.3	(66.9)	25.0
1996	808.3	179.0	64.6	630.7	(65.9)	25.0
1997	836.1	183.3	67.3	650.6	(65.1)	25.0
1998	864.5	187.7	70.0	671.0	(64.2)	25.0
1999	893.6	192.2	72.8	691.8	(63.3)	25.0
2000	923.5	196.8	75.8	713.2	(62.2)	25.0
2001	954.0	201.5	78.8	735.0	(61.3)	25.0
2002	985.0	206.3	81.9	757.4	(60.6)	25.0
2003	1019.5	211.2	83.8	780.3	(55.9)	25.0
2004	1055.1	216.2	85.8	803.8	(50.7)	25.0
2005	1091.8	221.3	87.8	827.8	(45.1)	25.0
2006	1126.0	226.6	89.7	852.3	(42.6)	25.0
2007	1160.9	232.0	91.7	877.3	(40.2)	25.0
2008	1196.6	237.5	93.8	902.8	(37.5)	25.0
2009	1232.8	243.0	95.8	928.7	(34.8)	25.0
2010	1269.5	248.6	97.9	955.1	(32.1)	25.0

Sources: BEA and NPA Data Services, Inc.

GROSS INVESTMENT
(Bill. 1982 $)

Year	Gross Investment	Fixed Nonresidential Investment	Fixed Residential Investment	Net Foreign Investment*
1950	210.7	124.0	86.7	-8.2
1951	204.3	131.7	72.6	23.9
1952	201.8	130.6	71.2	-4.3
1953	213.8	140.0	73.8	-22.6
1954	217.4	137.6	79.8	-28.6
1955	243.5	151.1	92.4	-7.4
1956	244.8	160.4	84.4	19.2
1957	240.4	161.1	79.3	14.5
1958	224.9	143.9	81.0	-12.4
1959	253.8	153.6	100.2	-2.2
1960	252.7	159.4	93.3	12.5
1961	251.8	158.2	93.6	6.6
1962	272.4	170.2	102.2	0.9
1963	290.6	176.7	113.9	-0.1
1964	310.2	194.9	115.3	1.6
1965	341.8	227.6	114.2	-1.6
1966	353.6	250.4	103.2	-8.8
1967	345.6	245.0	100.6	-7.7
1968	370.7	254.5	116.2	-15.4
1969	385.1	269.7	115.4	8.9
1970	373.3	264.0	109.3	2.7
1971	399.6	258.3	141.3	-15.0
1972	443.6	277.0	166.6	-21.0
1973	480.7	317.3	163.4	22.5
1974	448.1	317.9	130.2	31.3
1975	396.1	281.2	114.9	-2.8
1976	431.4	290.6	140.8	1.7
1977	492.1	324.0	168.1	-23.9
1978	540.1	362.1	178.0	-10.9
1979	560.2	389.4	170.8	-6.0
1980	516.2	379.2	137.0	-3.4
1981	521.7	395.2	126.5	26.5
1982	471.8	366.7	105.1	-15.1
1983	510.4	361.1	149.3	-66.2
1984	596.1	425.2	170.9	-80.2
1985	627.9	453.5	174.4	-151.6
1986	634.1	438.4	195.7	-157.6
1987	650.3	455.5	194.8	-140.3
1988	687.9	493.8	194.1	-110.0
1989	703.3	508.8	194.6	-49.7
1990	727.5	528.3	199.2	-57.4
1991	749.6	547.5	202.1	-55.5
1992	766.1	559.9	206.2	-44.3
1993	788.4	578.0	210.5	-36.7
1994	810.5	596.2	214.3	-32.1
1995	831.9	613.6	218.3	-25.8
1996	854.0	631.8	222.3	-20.7
1997	877.1	650.8	226.3	-15.9
1998	900.6	670.2	230.4	-11.1
1999	924.5	689.9	234.5	-5.9
2000	948.8	710.1	238.7	-0.3
2001	973.7	730.7	243.0	5.3
2002	998.9	751.5	247.4	11.2
2003	1024.7	772.9	251.8	19.8
2004	1050.0	793.6	256.3	30.1
2005	1075.7	814.8	260.9	41.1
2006	1101.9	836.3	265.6	49.1
2007	1127.5	857.2	270.3	58.3
2008	1154.0	878.9	275.1	67.5
2009	1181.0	901.0	279.9	76.8
2010	1208.1	923.2	284.8	86.5

* Calculated as a residual. Includes changes in business inventories and statistical discrepancy.

Sources: BEA and NPA Data Services, Inc.

National Planning Association

NPA is an independent, private, nonprofit, nonpolitical organization that carries on research and policy formulation in the public interest. NPA was founded during the Great Depression of the 1930s when conflicts among the major economic groups—business, labor, agriculture—threatened to paralyze national decision-making on the critical issues confronting American society. It was dedicated to the task of getting these diverse groups to work together to narrow areas of controversy and broaden areas of agreement as well as to map out specific programs for action in the best traditions of a functioning democracy. Such democratic and decentralized planning, NPA believes, involves the development of effective governmental and private policies and programs not only by official agencies but also through the independent initiative and cooperation of the main private sector groups concerned. To preserve and strengthen American political and economic democracy, the necessary government actions have to be consistent with, and stimulate the support of, a dynamic private sector.

NPA brings together influential and knowledgeable leaders from business, labor, agriculture, and the applied and academic professions to serve on policy committees. These committees identify emerging problems confronting the nation at home and abroad and seek to develop and agree upon policies and programs for coping with them. The research and writing for these committees are provided by NPA's professional staff and, as required, by outside experts.

In addition, NPA's professional staff undertakes research designed to provide data and ideas for policymakers and planners in government and the private sector. These activities include research on national goals and priorities, productivity and economic growth, welfare and dependency problems, employment and manpower needs, and technological change; analyses and forecasts of changing international realities and their implications for U.S. policies; and analyses of important new economic, social and political realities confronting American society. In developing its staff capabilities, NPA has increasingly emphasized two related qualifications. First is the interdisciplinary knowledge required to understand the complex nature of many real-life problems. Second is the ability to bridge the gap between theoretical or highly technical research and the practical needs of policymakers and planners in government and the private sector.

All NPA reports are authorized for publication in accordance with procedures laid down by the Board of Trustees. Such action does not imply agreement by NPA board or committee members with all that is contained therein unless such endorsement is specifically stated.

66

Selected NPA Publications

The Growth of Regional Trading Blocs in the Global Economy, ed. Richard S. Belous and Rebecca S. Hartley (168 pp, 1990, $15.00), NPA #243.

Continental Divide: The Values and Institutions of the United States and Canada, by Seymour Martin Lipset (326 pp, 1989, $13.00), CAC #59.

Dealing with the Budget Deficit, by Rudolph G. Penner (52 pp, 1989, $5.00), NAR #4.

On Preserving Shared Values. A British-North American Committee Statement on the 40th Anniversary of the Signing of the North Atlantic Treaty (16 pp, 1989, $2.00), BN #37.

The Contingent Economy: The Growth of the Temporary, Part-Time and Subcontracted Workforce, by Richard S. Belous (136 pp, 1989, $15.00), NPA #239.

Positioning Agriculture for the 1990s: A New Decade of Change. Symposium Papers sponsored by the Agribusiness Council of the Chamber of Commerce of Greater Kansas City and the Food and Agriculture Committee of the National Planning Association (160 pp, 1989, $12.00), FAC #7.

The 1992 Challenge from Europe: Development of the European Community's Internal Market, by Michael Calingaert (164 pp, 1988, $15.00), NPA #237.

The GATT Negotiations 1986-1990: Origins, Issues and Prospects, by Sidney Golt (120 pp, 1988, $10.00), BN #36.

Reassessing American Competitiveness, by Peter Morici (176 pp, 1988, $15.00), CIR #19.

New Departures in Industrial Relations: Developments in the U.S., the U.K. and Canada, An Occasional Paper (78 pp, 1988, $7.00), BN-OP #5.

Meeting the Competitive Challenge: Canada and the United States in the Global Economy, by Peter Morici (68 pp, 1988, $8.00), CAC #58.

Employment of Natural Scientists and Engineers: Recent Trends and Prospects, by Nestor E. Terleckyj (80 pp, 1986, $25.00), NPA #224.

NPA Membership is $65.00 per year, tax deductible. In addition to new NPA publications, members receive *Looking Ahead*, a quarterly journal, which is also available at the separate subscription price of $35.00. NPA members, upon request, may obtain a 30 percent discount on other publications in stock. A list of publications will be provided upon request. Quantity discounts are given.

Canada-U.S. Outlook, published quarterly by NPA, is available through a separate subscription rate of $20.00 per year.

NPA is a qualified nonprofit, charitable organization under section 501(c)(3) of the Internal Revenue Code.

NATIONAL PLANNING ASSOCIATION
1424 16th Street, N.W., Suite 700
Washington, D.C. 20036
Tel (202)265-7685 Fax (202)797-5516